POETRY
FOR THE
SOUL

POETRY
FOR THE
SOUL

Plus Satire

JEAN FRADENBURG MCPHEE

ARPress
ILLUMINATING IDEAS
EMPOWERING VOICES

ARPress
45 Dan Road Suite 5
Canton MA 02021

| Hotline: | 1(888) 821-0229 |
| Fax: | 1(508) 545-7580 |

Ordering Information:

Quantity sales. Special discounts are available on quantity purchases by corporations, associations, and others. For details, contact the publisher at the address above.

Printed in the United States of America.

ISBN-13:	Softcover	979-8-89330-377-3
	eBook	979-8-89330-378-0
	Hardcover	979-8-89356-209-5

Library of Congress Control Number: 2024902540

CONTENTS

INTRODUCTION

This poetry is for your soul.
Its words are meant to make you whole.
The Word, a gift from Creator God,
Who also came on earth to trod,
To lead you back toward the Lord
So that you, too, can be restored.
Your tears can wash your sin away.
In God's own peace, you can then stay.
The thief on the cross had only to say,
"Remember me, Lord," to be saved.
Not one of us is so depraved
That God's own hand cannot lift up
All who've tasted sorrow's cup.
When you've come to the end of you,
God's miracle can then come true.
The Holy Ghost is God on earth,
Who fills you after your new birth.

A TRUE MIRACLE (TESTIMONY)

Once many years ago,
Driving back from the beach,
Cars were not going slow,
And the bridge gave no breach.
The Three Mile Bridge was two lanes wide,
And cars were rolling on every side.
Just behind me was an eighteen-wheel truck,
And a new eerie noise meant the end of my luck.
I knew at once that danger was there,
But no way to stop with a truck looming tall,
And a bridge not yet widened gave no room to spare.
A crash would soon come if the car had to stall.
There was no way out, so I started to pray,
"Lord, keep us going; there's still a long way."
Out of three miles, still halfway to go.
A mile and a half, and I could not slow.
Traffic was heavy, and the truck was at full speed.
There was no escape if the Lord did not heed.
The noise was horrendous, and it did not fade,
Yet the car kept on rolling until I had made
The end of the bridge and a chance to pull over.
The noise had now stopped, but not my concern.
What had it been? So, I jumped out to learn.
Ribbons of rubber 'round a rim bare of tire.
The rim on the concrete had made all that noise,
But how had I made it? A power that's higher?
I stood there astonished and lacking all poise.
When up pulled a car, and the driver hopped out,
Gave me my hubcap and turned back about.
The bearded man was soon on his way,

Leaving me speechless with nothing to say.
I then concluded angels just do their job,
With no word spoken, the silence to rob.
As the car sped away, I saw on his plate,
"In God we trust" from the Alabama state.
I was still amazed the car made it at all,
But now, with my hubcap, I soon made a call.
I'll have the car towed, for the rim must be ruined.
The source of the noise was now clear, all clues in,
Yet this miracle still had a sequel,
No damaged rim, much without equal.
I am blessed to receive the gift of God's grace;
All who call on His name can receive the same.
His mercy is new every day,
And He saves in every way
Those who come under His sway.

DO IT NOW

It's far more pleasant to live in the present
That's not hard to grasp; don't hold onto the past.
When you let go at last,
You are free to become more than all you're freed from.
Ah, new you, it's true! There is more than you ever knew.
Can you learn to forgive?
Bad thoughts from the past can be banished at last.
Then your heart is set free to be all you can be.
God forgives you, too,
For His mercy is just.
In this, you can trust.
Once you free others,
You gain countless brothers.
God's Spirit will stay,
When you follow His way.
Believe! Receive! Don't be deceived!
You've been reprieved.
It is surely so, so never let go.
Your own freedom will flow; true peace you will know.
Hallelujah! Amen! You're beginning again!
Your rebirth is real, so embrace what you feel.

FORGIVE AND FORGET

৶

Forgiveness is a blessing and not a sacrifice.
God's way removes all stressing, and frees us from sinful lice
That hideaway, controlling an equally sinful itch
To recall all ancient memories and never lose a stitch
Of all assorted patterns that recall bad thoughts to you
For all bad thoughts bring with them your ancient feelings, too.
You will relive the anger; you will relive the pain;
You will face sudden danger of suffering once again.
But worse than that, you're still enraged
By bad emotions from your cage.
Your family and your friends receive
The brunt of all and soon believe
That you are a source of anger, that you are a source of fear.
They will suffer from your memories, and seldom want you near.
Forgive and forget; do not retain
What causes you and others pain.
When the spirit of God is in you,
You can do what you could not do.

Therefore, as the elect of God, holy and beloved, put on tender mercies,
kindness, humility, meekness, longsuffering; bearing with one another...
if anyone has a complaint against another; even as Christ forgave you,
so you also must do.

But above all these things put on love, which is the bond of perfection.
[Not romantic, erotic love but agape love of self-sacrifice, even as Christ
did for you.]

And let the peace of God rule in your hearts, to which also you were called in one body; and be thankful.

Colossians 3:12–15 (NKJV)

Since Christ's blood washes sinners clean,
We're blessed that we may intervene.
We surrender all before His throne,
And share the mercy we have known.

FORGIVENESS

Those who ponder most on the offenses of others,
Mask the love of their Father, who created them brothers.
If you wait for others to say, "I'm wrong,"
Your heart remains in a prison so strong.
God wants you to have peace by first,
Freeing your heart from what is worst.
Holding onto bitter thoughts
Can harm your own soul, waiting on "oughts."
The other "ought" to say he's wrong,
But you can be first to sing freedom's song.
God's mercy can wash away the grime,
Even if another committed the crime.
What the devil doesn't want you to know
Is that God's spirit frees your soul to grow
Into His likeness who died for you,
Forgiving all you could ever do.
An excerpt from God's ABCs, created by inspiration.

GOD'S CHILDREN

The child who complains
Is the child bound by pain.
It loops like a rope,
Entangling your hope.
The child who can praise
Sees that beauty abounds.
God's glory can raise
Us beyond what surrounds.
The child who knows joy
Can survive all attacks.
God's peace will destroy
Thoughts that anger brings back.
The child who forgives
Sets his own soul free.
He eternally lives
And helps others to see.

GOD'S WORD

True Jews, Christians, and Muslims, too,
Know honor to God's Word is due.

Exodus 14:14 (NASB),
"The LORD will fight for you, while you keep silent."

God seeks not slaves but friends indeed,
When truth rules rather than a creed;
Men's minds can never overrule
What God uses prophets to reveal.
If men change truth, it is not true.
Yet the enemy ever seeks to steal
Our blessings from our living God,
Who once came on this earth to trod.
When God gives Himself as our greatest gift,
We can see beyond the devil's rift.
God's Spirit can fill our very soul;
We are restored, and love reigns whole.
God proved His love by sacrifice.
It is in giving that we live twice.
For earth below cannot compare
To heaven where there's no despair.
None can blind us to eternal life,
Prepared once we surrender strife.
Amid all our commotion,
Death is our promotion.

Those dying with prayer on their lips
Receive mercy for their many slips.
Those living lonely on their own
Have narrow souls that have not grown
To the peace and power of life renewed
By our God who came to end all feuds.
There is none so blind as he who will not see,
The path God planned wins victory.
The devil rules with hate and fear,
God's grace makes both sins disappear.
How do we win the war with sin?
Once we forgive, we've truly learned to live.

BLACK AND WHITE

⁓

When it comes to bright, we can know the dark,
But concerning people, shadows will lurk.
I've seldom seen a skin tone truly kin to white,
And seldom is a skin so black we cannot see the light.
For tones of tan are everywhere, and tans are often sought.
Why then do we extol extremes when that's not what we ought?
For God so blends the human race that we cannot call pure,
As God amends the human flaws that cease not but endure.
Once we admit we are from God,
We clear our lenses, drop our rods,
For peace within is better far
Than "peace" that follows human war.
The whiter your skin,
The more likely you'll learn
That the darker your skin,
The less likely you'll burn.
That also applies to white wrinkles track
'Cause it's widely known that "black don't crack."

BLACK LIVES MATTER

Who cares if a few are sacrificed to the cause of world dominion?
Communist organizers know riots help to sway opinion.
That black children suffer for unholy protest
Does not seem to matter; they are sacrificed for the "best."
The "best," however, seems not to come
By free choice or democratic vote.
Somehow people can be really dumb.
They prefer independence to rule by rote.
Ownership by all is possession by none.
Rulers are owners at their beck and call.
All that you ever earned is done.
We have the freest nation on earth
Since God gives free will, Who gave us birth,
Socialist parties delete "under God."
They know their new God, the state, seems odd.
Black lives matter, yes, they do,
But so do policemen, too.
To paint all with a single brush
Is as unfair as communism's crush.
Communism, socialism for new slaves
Since when the few are ruling with power,
The many have no rights to save.
Beware of such a thunderous shower.
We'll find we must obey new rules,
Enforced by power of oppressive tools.

FANNY LOU

⌒

God clearly uses women, too,
For slavery shows that power rules.
The weaker vessels must be broken,
When men believe their strength has spoken.
Yet God teaches from an eternal view,
For moral corruption is nothing new.
Men even claimed that God decreed
Segregation to be a moral deed.
Fannie Lou spoke out, for truth has power
To unveil lies that protect cowards.
Cowards believe that might makes right,
But truth proclaims another light,
"This little light of mine
I'm gonna let it shine,"
Sang out a woman led by God,
Who did not fear the coward's rod!
Mississippi was mostly black.
So, whites feared their vote was an attack
On what they saw as moral right
To burn their crosses in the night.
Why did they veil white faces with hoods?
The devil disguises bad as good.
Why did they hang blacks upon a tree?
Their Savior came thus to set men free.
God's ways are far above our own,
But heaven, in the end, atones

For all the suffering the weak must face,
For their strength shines even in disgrace.
God Himself came to suffer the same,
But in the end, death will reclaim
The justice God's mercy overcame:
God's truth gives time to look above
To see that suffering is a form of love
That is stronger far than might of men,
For there's an eternal night for those
Who never find the light that rose
To shine above the cross's pain,
And so, proclaim another reign:
One eternal far from earthly strife,
For those who learn death leads to life,
Or to the pain of separation
From the God who came for reparation.
"Those who were last will be the first" (Luke 13:30, NKJV,
paraphrased).
First on earth proves to be the worst.
The time will come
And it's very soon.
When God's truth will prove
The greatest boon.
Small minds cannot conceive
Of anything greater
Than human beings.

"FREE AT LAST!"
"FREE AT LAST!"

✑

In honor of the God and Savior of Martin Luther King.
If God gives you a neighbor, is stealing a sin?
Would God give you the right to steal from him?
The spirit of slavery demands that you steal,
But the spirit of freedom will strengthen and heal.
The spirit of slavery claims freedom to kill,
But the spirit of freedom blesses free will.
The spirit of slavery encourages hate,
But the spirit of freedom gives strength for your fate.
For God blesses freedom and allows you to choose,
But those who steal freedom are destined to lose.
Heaven's gate slams firmly shut on all who hate, steal and lie,
But Jesus will welcome true believers on high.
God gives you true freedom to end tyranny's lie,
He gives free choice to choose Him and not die.
On the anniversary of Martin Luther King's ascension.

GOD BLESS AMERICA

An aged lady spoke to me; her gray hairs gave her grace.
I listened to her words, so free, so full of fervor like her race.
"I might be workin' like a slave,
But my young'uns will do better.
God is with me when I pray…
The Word of God like my own letter."
"He who works not should not eat.
That don't mean just for wages
My goal's to see Satan's defeat
'Cause he deceives in lyin' stages."
Step by step, we're led astray,
'Til someone will stand up for right.
God's David has a little stone,
But it's slung from the Rock of Ages.
God loves each sister and brother, too,
But the God of peace wants us to fight.
God will bless America if we do our part.
Each small vote what's not of God surely hurts His heart."

THE CENTRAL PARK FIVE: THE CRIME OF THE CENTURY TRANSFORMED BY GODLY MERCY

∽

The Central Park Five were finally freed,
For their testimony had never agreed,
But that didn't stop them from serving time.
They were in prison, though their DNA did not rhyme
The lies each told against his brothers,
Included each as witnesses against the others.
The police used twenty-four-hour interrogation
To prompt the details they would ration:
Each lie they told came back on them,
Including themselves in all the mayhem.
The devil really laughed with glee.
The police implied that some could go free,
Only if they gave stories that somewhat agreed.
Yet the truth they missed was that their lies
Gave evidence of a crime to be despised,
And the victim was barely still alive.
It seemed the crime of the century,
In Central Park, black teens on a spree
With stones beat a homeless man,
Harassed bike riders as part of the plan.
So, adding a rape with a beaten body
Seemed no stretch at all to the public body.
Black teens on a rampage group rape white female
Alone out jogging on a Central Park trail:
Lies prompted by police to "save their own lives."
Wound up making the five of all most despised.
The police used twenty-four-hour interrogation

To prompt the details they would ration
Each lie they told came back on them,
Including themselves in all the mayhem.
How then did the five finally go free?
The victim survived, but no memory.
It was now not a murder, only beating and rape,
But they still had a miraculous escape.
The real rapist had murdered several others,
Was in the same prison with one of the brothers.
They had a spat, but this one the brother forgave
Said, "It's nothing, man," and forgave him his rage.
A guilty conscience convicted the rapist, sharing his cage.
Another suffered for his crime with no escape;
He was the one who'd performed all the rapes.
He then told others he hated to understand
An innocent man was jailed for his own reprimand.
The truth revealed then was verified;
The young men had been coached into their lies.
The truth revealed corrected the media, too.
Who made stories wilder than what teens really do.
They had lied to keep lives somewhat healed,
But their lies were corrected by truth revealed.
A forgiving brother saved all five,
For the real killer repented to save their lives.
Forgiveness has power, but many declined
To believe the truth once really defined.
The truth revealed many never admitted.
Prejudice remained though all five were acquitted.

A GARDEN, A GIFT

To receive a garden you did not own
Is to know true blessings from God's throne.
To receive a garden you think you have earned
Is to show how little you have learned.
God made the garden, then made it grow.
He gave you free choice to be blind or to know
That every flower is the work of His power,
That there is drought when God is left out.
When the Word of God is rare,
When people turn from prayer,
Their gardens are overcome with weeds;
Their gardens will reflect their deeds,
There is only one way that is right:
God gave His Word to guide your sight.
The devil is real and will deceive
If you have no power to believe.
Those who forget God forget what they owe
To seek only the moment of pleasure.
They eat from the garden but forget it must grow.
They deny they were given a treasure.

A NEW SONG

Give God your life
And be free from strife.
Renounce all your wrong
And you'll hear His song:
You know how to flow
In the Spirit, so,
Keep your inner glow
And your love light burning.
There is no returning to the devil's Day
Once God shows the way.
Praise the Lord!
Praise, the best reward
For all who come your way,
Whenever the Word
Directs all you say.
God's Word points the way
To a better day,
God came down to heal,
Saying, "Peace. Be still.
Know that I am God
And I spare the rod."
As He sows His seed,
We reap joy indeed.
Before you die,
He will hear your cry.
Believe and so receive.

He welcomes home the late
And saves us from our fate.
God can cleanse all sin.
Live the Word to win.
His restoring grace
Will the wrong erase;
All that led you wrong
Helps you learn His song:
God can still save me;
I can be set free,
Even my wrong choice
Clarifies His voice.

GOD KNOWS

We do not know what God thinks of us,
In our minds, bad thoughts don't cause us to fuss.
We dismiss them as secrets not known to any,
Yet God knows each bad thought, and there are many.
We have not robbed any bank, so we think,
Yet God knows our jealous desires on the brink.
When we want what others have, we observe:
We think we should have what we really deserve.
God counts thoughts as sin, which we never have done.
Angry rage kept within is the same thing as sin.
We're only kidding when we undress, just for fun,
The handsome and beautiful, as if we were one.
God came to earth to tell the truth fully,
When we think sinful thoughts, we are playing the bully.
We do not murder, so we feel so clean,
But a murderous thought is as if it had been.
We do not deceive anyone but our own selves,
When we think we are better than those in jail cells.

HEALING A BROKEN HEART

A broken heart begins the healing,
For godly sorrow is God's revealing.
There's surely a way to forgive what men say.
And women as well can learn to laugh truly,
Since there's just one right way,
And all wrongs are unruly.
They spread like a mesh
That traps us in stress.
But peace is far stronger
and eternity longer.
God's peace can come now.
In God's truth, you'll know how.
When your heart opens wide,
No more sin can divide.
Your heart can be healed,
When God's mercy is sealed.
A poet lives in inner space.
Still, all wrongs can be erased.
Sometimes even he can spy
The truth told in a flower that dies.
No longer what rules
Are your sad thoughts the tools,
For they can be washed clean:
Mercy overcomes mean.
For the ways of the cross
Are all gain and no loss.

For God's kingdom is strong,
Right prevails over wrong.
For you can be set free
When you climb on His tree.
The mighty rolling of the sea,
Wave on wave overpowers me.
The truth rolls on ever, on and on,
But lies will perish, going, going gone.

"HE WHO SEEKS WILL FIND"

Christians know some truth,
But not all of it:
Unless God lives within,
You have not escaped sin.
Hindus know some truth,
But not all of it:
Once we learn to pray,
We are finding our way.
Moslems know some truth,
But not all of it,
For God lives within
When we die to ourselves.
Free choice is God's gift,
But not force that veils.
Atheists know some truth,
But not all of it:
God gave us free choice
That we might hear His voice.
Devil worshippers have discovered a lie,
For the devil hates truth,
And he wants you to die.

JESUS AT THE LAKE OF GALILEE

The old boat neared the shore,
Coming straight at us.
We saw the mast it bore,
With bare, well-formed crossbar.
It formed the perfect cross,
An empty one.
Dear Lord, you saw it staged,
The cross that was to come.
Each fishing boat your passage
To the day when all was done.
No one else could see the sign
Coming toward the shore.
The crossbar of the mast
Would become an open door.

THE MIRROR

There is a mind; there is a heart,
But are they so really far apart?
Here's a test that you can use.
You'll know the truth unless you refuse.
Once you're offended, you can think the worse,
Yet God says forgive, and don't rehearse
The same old memories, time after time,
For anger masks joy, and your heart won't rhyme.
Once you obey and set your mind free
By releasing each painful memory,
Then you feel the peace within that God desires.
The Holy Spirit resides when you do as God requires.
God's spirit cannot remain
When evil thinking is retained:
Remembering the wrongs of others
Prevents your focus on men as brothers.
You, too, have transgressed,
But you'll forget your mess
If you seek to be the judge,
You are playing God when you begrudge
The same mercy to them He extends to you.
That choice is something you cannot do:
If you seek forgiveness, you must forgive.
There's no way you can transgress and live.
Eternal peace in heaven begins on earth.
If you've closed heaven's doors, you'll feel the dearth,

For peace and joy and harmony
Are gifts when God has set you free.
Now you can begin to see
That what you think brings victory:
Once your thoughts have turned to good,
Your heartfelt feelings have lifted the hood.
When your feelings repress you,
Change your mind.
You'll find depression is a waste.
Once you peel the outer rind,
The fruit within is free to taste.
Once you peel away your angry thoughts,
Your inner heart relaxes as it ought.
When you change your thoughts, you change your mind:
Your heart's mirror, a new reflection finds
What you think is what you'll feel.
Emotions are but mirrors real.
Once you know the truth of this,
To choose by feelings is amiss.

THE PRICE OF AMERICA

❦

Some of us were raised on John Wayne.
Some were raised on video games.
All of us have a T-shirt at hand.
Most have jeans with tight waistbands.
We've always had freedom to protest,
But Selma showed us at our best,
At using government against its own,
For freedom's won, not just bestowed.
We're blessed when leaders tell the truth.
We're blessed when leaders are willing to die.
We're cursed when leaders are uncouth.
We're cursed when leaders live a lie.
We're proudest when we take a stand,
Since actions, not words, make the man.
We follow when we forget to fight,
For there are causes that are right.
We spend with credit card delight,
Until we learn the price that bites.
We're all for one and one for all
When our own team takes a fall.
We look forward to the coming year,
Even if change is cause for fear.
Though it's the land of opportunity,
In the end, we have a common enemy:
Our own comfort can make us shirk.
If we truly believe, then we must work.

It's a myth that we deserve to retire:
There's a fight to the finish that's required.
We have only ourselves to blame,
If the next generation proves too lame.
Our country will only preserve our rights,
If we keep the cost within our sights.
Divorce and desertion lead to death,
Though we have not paused to take a breath.
Freedom, we know, is never free
We must take responsibility.

THE REVELATION OF OUR GOD TO JOHN

This is too much for my little mind.
Let me but glean what I can find.
When Jesus speaks, the Word is clear,
For all deception disappears.

"I am the Alpha and the Omega"
And I am "the Beginning and the End"

(Revelation 1:8a, NKJV).

No one will have to puzzle or beg,
For He is the Word on which we depend.
Jesus came to suffer for us.
His truth echoed in John's chorus:

"The Word was with God, and the Word was God"

(John 1:1, NKJV).

"He who has seen Me has seen the Father"

(John 14:9, NKJV).

"I am in the Father, and the Father in me."
When you see Me, you see Him.
Jesus asked, "Do you not believe that I am in the Father, and the Father in Me?"

(John 14:10, 11, NKJV).

To mortal eyes, He's the lamb that was slain.
Sacrifice through the ages proclaiming He came.
Earthly fathers are separate from their sons,
But God's own Spirit is all in One.
Unity is hard for mortal men,
For our minds cannot begin to comprehend
To conceive the Creator of all that lives.
We see the world by what He gives,
Whose miracle moments our souls uplift
Beyond understanding of the gift.
Our coming together can result in birth,
But knowing the process exceeds our worth.
We can no more create a sperm
Than we can escape from every germ.
We are far better at delivering death,
For all it takes is cessation of breath.
But God can deliver from death as well,
Once we know our truths are His to tell.

The Revelation ends as it began, Testifying God's truth to mortal man
"I am the Alpha and the Omega"

(John 22:13, NKJV)

God came to earth walking on legs.
He is "the Beginning and the End."
Our gift of life on Him depends
Our God is "the First and the Last"

(Revelation 22:13, NKJV)

"Morning Star" to our homeward path

(Revelation 22:16, NKJV)

"If you had known Me, you would have known My Father also; and from now on you know Him and have seen Him"

(John 14:7, NKJV)

"And he who sees Me sees Him who sent Me"

(John 12:45, NKJV)

"Hear, O Israel: The LORD our God, the LORD is one!"

(Deuteronomy 6:4, NKJV)

TRUTH IN LOVE

◦∾◦

"Immortal, invisible, God only wise" (1 Timothy 1:17).

Eternally reigns in the highest of skies,
Lord Jesus, we thank you for coming to earth,
For leaving your heaven to prove our true worth.
The Lord, our Creator, who gave us our souls,
Restores us to greater life when we're whole.
The time now for trial lets temptation rule,
Yet the short time of trial reveals time as a tool.
Eternity beckons for those who are wise,
But damnation threatens those who live lies.
God's kingdom is truth, and those enter in
When deception uncouth is revealed to be sin.
God's kingdom of mercy is extended to all
Who, in turn, will show mercy to others who fall.
For those who hurt others and entice them away
Have lost the rich blessing of those who can pray.
The path that leads homeward restores our souls to God.
The path that leads downward maligns truth as odd.
For truth is still holy, and humans are able
To find they act boldly when fed at His table.
Christ taught us communion, for we needed no more
Than present reunion with all that restores.
Once we know true joy, no other pleasure will do.
Once we seek to employ God's love, we are true.
With no other vision and no other goal
Than to fulfill our mission to help others be whole.
Truth, love, and mercy give grace to the blind.

There is no better hope than to have peace of mind.
To be one with God, there's no better goal.
Why gain the whole world and still ruin your soul?
Why seek only forgetting when you could be made whole?
Earth's address is no longer needed when
God's word is heeded.
Time will reverse, and you will rehearse
All you've ever done or thought, unless
by blood you've been bought.
Then, if Jesus takes your case,
all your sins will be erased.
If Jesus is your chosen Lord, you'll
receive what you could not afford.
Your good deeds are far too few, but Jesus
paid the price for you.
A shining light will show the way, and then,
at last, you're home to stay.
A brand-new life you will begin once
earthly days have reached their end.
This is a promise, tried and true,
for God Himself will welcome you.
All your sorrow will flee away, for heaven's
joy will come to stay.
Before time began, He made the earth,
then came to show You your rebirth.
After death, you will remain His friend;
after His death, He rose again.
None other ever made this claim;
He died to free you from your blame.
God's love eternal provided proof;
His Word eternal is the truth.

WITH OR WITHOUT GOD

With God, you can have perfect peace.
Fear and worry will simply cease.
His promise is heaven,
No death at all.
His promise: forgiveness,
Whenever you fall.

What is the secret to this mystery?
God ruling your life will set you free.
It is a free choice you must make.
Give up troubles and joys that are fake.
When you give God full control,
True peace and joy will fill your soul.
Why live insecurely and "hit and miss"?
God's promise is even more than this.

"The LORD will fight for you, and you shall hold your peace"

(Exodus 14:14, NKJV)

The Lord will protect us better
than ever we can.
For even in the worst of times,
He can perfect His plan.
We're all in transformation,
More peace and joy to find.
Our spirits lightened thus will soar
above the loads we've ceased to mind.
Once we're releasing all offense,
we become like Him, so mercifully kind.

CHILDREN, CHILDREN

Children, children, grow up fast,
If you want freedom to last.
Politicians want your wealth,
By spending what you earn through stealth.
Even before you earn a dime,
Your taxes have begun to climb.
No family can live well in debt,
For the price to pay is coming yet.
So, a nation that consumes its wealth,
By causing debt steals children's health.
How hard will they have to have worked
To pay the national debt their parents shirked?
Who then is left to pay the bill
When debt is mounting on the hill?
Only the children pay for what's "free,"
For they inherit debt, you see.
Children, children, grow up fast,
If you want your wealth to last.

DEBTORS

We each owe so much to others.
Why disdain to call them brothers?
Did you construct the house you own?
Who hewed the wood? Who laid the stone?
Did you grow the grain you eat for bread?
Did you weave the carpet on which you tread?
Did you milk the cow to make ice cream?
Did you write the book that lets you dream?
Did you make the child that you call yours,
Or was that miracle a grace that lures
You into love Who makes family and friends?
Did you make the water on which life depends?
Did you ever imagine all you owe?
How then believe all was yours to blow?
Do you see now what debt is yours?
Who gave you the light of a day that endures?
Who gave you that life you call your own?
Do you not believe that God is on the throne?
Do you not believe your parents gave birth?
Do you not believe in this miracle earth?
One planet among the countless stars.
One planet more fine-tuned than your car.
In the quiet of early morning prayer,
The heart will speak. No silence there.
When God fills our very souls,
We're never alone. We've been made whole.

CHANGE

Is it best to feel our way through life,
Or get light to see reality?
Do we choose the difficult way of strife,
Or choose to check out unity?
There seems so much to rearrange.
But perhaps my viewpoint could stand change.
Let's try out what seems at first seems strange:
No danger in exploring points of view.
You may find understanding changes you.
Laughter is the very best cure:
You recognize the truth for sure.
Laughter is the very best sign,
Two separate views can realign.
Be open to another point of view,
You will find understanding changes you.
Laughter may be the best of clues
That new truth transforms you anew,
And lets you love others who differ from you.
Truth doesn't change, but it's good that we do.
Laughter is the very best sign,
Two separate views can realign.
Perhaps the truth can make us one,
As God, the Father is the Son.

DECLARATION OF INDEPENDENCE II

God says each one is free to choose,
But when the state is "god" all lose.
Biden says, "Sacrifice for the greater good."
But the greater good is misunderstood,
Since "the greater good" is determined by men
Whose rule from the top is a colossal flop.
How efficient can it be?
For it all depends on you and me
When each takes responsibility.
True efficiency comes when you're free,
Not when bureaucrats make the final rule,
Assuming the rest of us are fools;
Fools to follow dictates of others
When we know all men are brothers:
Brothers free to make decisions,
Not bowing to government precision.
God alone gives us free choice,
So how can our rulers claim our voice?
We have had the freest nation on earth
To lose that right would bring sad birth:
Sacrifice of full-term babies to harvest organs
Makes all of us guilty of choices forgone.
If we are now forlorn,
If we don't want the feds to rule,
Then we are free when rulers play the fool.
All new inventions come from new thoughts,

Not from men in charge issuing "oughts."
Rule the rulers; let them understand
That states make the rules that govern our land.
Then our country will do more than "survive."
By God's blessing, we will thrive.
Poets for freedom and victory.

YOUR BOOK

God fills each day with beauty;
You only have to look.
God then calls nights to duty,
Spangling the dark with spark-like hooks
To draw eyes Godward to His book.
He writes with myriad weathers
And clouds that drop their dews.
So go forth, but glance down rather,
For each step reveals His clues.
All stars like dust were scattered
In perfect braille to teach the blind.
The dark that really mattered
Paints the promise to refine.
As stars recede, we learn to pray
For a clearer view on another day.

YOUR FREE CHOICE

⌒

God's perfect call is open to all.
He awaits your invitation
To come in and reign.
What will you lose?
All you call pain.
What will you gain?
Perfect peace that remains.
Even when troubles come forward again,
All former doubts become perfectly plain.
Even then, His way surpasses your own,
Even when you surrender your throne.
Even when you refuse to take back
All of the problems that led to your lack,
Even when others pretend to be brothers,
Even when others refuse to remain,
Even then, you know your fears are at rest.
Even when Satan sends others to test,
Even then, you will find manifest
That God as your guide brings all of His best.
May you find the way to be heavenly blest:
Whenever trials try to bring stress,
His presence within overcomes all the rest.

CONTROL FROM THE TOP? WHAT A FLOP!

We do not now intend to lose
The freedom for each one to choose,
The freedom for valid votes to count,
Not allowing mail-in fraud to mount.
All creators should be free.
One good idea brings victory,
But let's be sure the truth prevails,
And double-check results that fail.
Those bent on securing their own places
Don't serve the best for any races.
Those who choose others instead,
Will honor our heritage from the dead,
Who risked their lives for freedom's sake,
Who suffered for the right to take,
Charge of their own children's lives.
Not subject them to a godless state,
Nor mere propaganda's prize
That cares not for the unborn's fate.

FREE ELECTIONS / FAIR ELECTIONS

∽

All I want for Christmas is a fair election.
Evidence of fraud has not escaped detection.
The media responds in the same old way:
Sold out to the far left to our deep dismay.
Authorize a revote for fraud against the law,
Or throw out wrong results that daily clench our jaw.
We cannot call democracy vote based on fraud.
We cancel our democracy when fraud is lauded.
We cancel our democracy when the count's not right.
We cancel our democracy with votes by night.
We want legislatures to right this wrong.
Pledge money to correct what mars our song.
We no longer have "sweet land of liberty"
Because of forced results by crime against the free.
We're free to right the wrong when fraud defames our song.
Count by hand whenever machine programs lie.
Disdain the technology that counts awry.
Authorize a civil suit for crimes against this nation.
Authorize new deadlines that protect our nation.
One man, one vote.
One woman, one vote.
One citizen, one vote.
Not polls that lie, so freedom dies!
It is socialism that robs;
Capitalism produces jobs.
For the sake of the ancestors and the unborn,

The living must defend freedom or be shorn
Like sheep.
Decide.
Do not let technology destroy what we have a right to employ:
Defense of our land. So, take a stand,
Or weep like sheep,
Shorn of legal rights we must fight to keep.
Like Esther,
If I die, I die.
God help us try.

Love in Christ,
Who tells us twice,
By word and deed,
What Christians should heed:
"Greater love has no one than this, than to lay down one's life for his
friends"

(John 15:13, NKJV)

TIME TO REGISTER TO VOTE

Should the long-dead be given roles,
When we vote and go to the polls?
Judicial watch has been suing long,
For Los Angeles to right this wrong.
One and a half million plus from their rolls, alone
Had to be purged when the truth emerged.
Can you imagine what crime still remains?
When many states have suits sustained,
Colorado, Pennsylvania, Virginia, too,
Join North Carolina in this famous queue.
If some honest lawyers are fighting for you,
What, as a citizen, should you do?
"Nothing" is one answer to this game.
But one day, you may be treated the same.
How long do you want to continue to vote,
Once in a casket that others must tote?
Perhaps you could make it clear in your will,
That you don't want to keep voting still.
Then, if they retain your name, it's not your fault,
You've done your best to clear out the vault.

NEW BIRTH

Only God can
Make us whole,
For God's control
Restores my soul.
Our bad beliefs
Give no relief.
Let such grief go,
And then, we'll know
Freedom at last
From all our past.
Let God reveal
His joy is real,
Freed from disguise
And all false highs.
New thoughts allow
True heaven now.
New birth began in unity,
We can forgive,
We are set free.
Our now becomes eternity.

SATAN'S LIES

Who but the devil desires to inspire fear?
That this is his favorite torture is clear.
Does not the devil seek to inspire hate?
Yet haters can't hide from their ultimate fate.
God, great in heaven, loves those who love.
He comes to earth with gifts from above.
But those who harm children are destined for shrouds:
God has no reward for those haughty or proud.
Shrouds do not protect from hot flames of hell.
Even death holds more terrors for warriors who fell.
God gives no warm welcome to heaven above
To those who wear masks to deceive those who love.
And how does the devil welcome his hosts?
He merely claims victory with his empty boasts.
The devil deceives, destroys, and discovers
That believers in hate destroy their own brothers.
Believers in hate have no true bonds of faith,
Are corrupting their hearts and demonically gifted.
Those raping the weak leave their own souls to be sifted.
You've one chance to repent since the true God forgives.
You've one chance to be freed from the
lies you now live.
For Jesus died to give life and is coming again,
But Mohammed discovered he misled his friends.
For the Koran still will witness to one virgin birth,
Yet blends truth with falsehood to give Satan mirth.

"Hurting people" still "hurt others, *" (*David Jeremiah, servant of God)
But Jesus came to make us brothers.
Because we are all God's own children,
The worst can become the best of men,
And the Son of man can forgive sin.
And God's Word can transform your soul,
Can heal your body and make you whole.
Father Abraham's test to surrender his son
Would foretell the great promise God made to all men:
"For God so loved the world that He gave His only begotten Son."

SPIRITUAL WARFARE

Poets are prophets
Who like rhythm and rhyme.
They pretend to tell truths,
But not all the time.
Birds sing.
Bees hum.
Bells ring.
Musicians strum.
We are led to imitate the best.
Yet demons try to intimidate the rest.
Some people come to clear the weeds.
Poetic license limits creeds.
Few there be who find the way.
Still, a warning comes to those who pray.

STAND WITH THE WORD

The devil has overplayed his hand,
And now, too clearly, all can see
That banning God throughout our land
Has proven to Christians that we're free:
Free to pray whenever God leads,
Free to share faith wherever God speeds,
Free to suffer whatever is hurled,
For our God sent Christ to save the world.
Even our enemies must declare
That Jesus lives in those who dare,
Just as our forebears crossed the sea
And sought freedom to live what they believed.
So, ought we to give from what we've received
The blessings we know outshine what we leave.
We, too, will reach out to native sons,
Give them our Bible with baptism won.
We'll melt the hearts that have gone stone cold,
For our God loves them enough to make our hearts bold.
That is what the Bible teaches me,
And our God has promised victory
When we are low, our God is high,
When we are weak, our God reigns ever,
When we speak, our Savior is nigh,
Whenever, wherever, whatever.
Inspired by the readings of His Word.

TWO MASTERS

Strife is of the enemy.
Peace is the blessing of the free.
The master of the universe rules well
All those freed from the devil's spell.
Though the ruler of this world loves to enslave,
One God alone frees from the grave.
There is joy below for those freed from sin.
There is joy above when their choices win.
The new life of true freedom is serving God,
Who makes good of ill and will spare the rod.
There are two masters, but one forms his slaves,
And one who sets us free from all that depraves.
You can surely know which one you serve:
The truly free have peace within.
The free find bliss again and again.
Yet all that enslaves the human will,
Is the spiral downward that passions fulfill.
You will see that suffering in God's grace
Is better than pleasure that leaves no trace.
The pleasure of the moment leads astray,
But the permanent joy of God's presence displays
A far higher height of human bliss
Than those betrayed by a transient kiss.
You can be warned and so transformed,
For our Savior came to still your storms.

WHAT, IN FACT, DO YOU HAVE TO LOSE?

The Giver of gifts will never refuse
To replace all that once tempted,
With blessings profuse.
You will be exempted and need no excuse,
When angels come calling,
To set your soul loose.
God will bless you and yours,
For His Power endures.
God is your Maker.
The Devil, the faker.
He will always lead astray
All who don't choose God's way.
Choose to become a child of the King:
Your new birth brings new songs to sing.
All of creation leads you to praise,
The path to elation guiding your days.
When mere happiness fades,
When the price becomes steep,
Eternal joy stays;
For others, you'll weep.
Be always amazed at new causes for praise.

WHO ARE YOU?

Do you define yourself, or are you clay?
Are you what you want to be, or in dismay?
Look in your heart of hearts to seek a void.
If you find emptiness, you're ill-employed.
It is not your destined goal to please a so-claimed friend,
For it is your own soul you must learn to defend.
How do you know who you truly are?
Until your Maker is not far,
You will weary yourself with vain pursuits;
You will not know peace or joy, to boot.
When your heart is truly glad, you don't desire.
When your heart is truly good, you don't require.
All your needs fulfilled can't be,
Until you find that love is free.
But know you have a mortal enemy.
There's a spirit world that you can't see.
Yet, in the flesh, you'll find no victory.
For the devil tempts with power to gain a slave,
Once, then, you're obsessed, you'll serve 'til the grave.
There's only one way you can break the chains:
Discover that your Maker can still reign.
God's given you free will, but the devil still knows.
If he can claim your choice, the wrong choice overthrows.
All the plans for good God has for you.
You're too blind to even find when you rule, too.
The devil shows Delilah as a lure.
You'll think that what pleases you can be your cure.
Once you believe the lie that you can't change,

You won't allow your God to wholly rearrange.
But bear in mind, once you decide sin doesn't satisfy,
You have a help to overcome the devil once you try.
For God above came here below just to claim his own.
There's not a sin He cannot wash; His blood will all atone.
All that you need is sorrow for wrong
choice that led astray.
God will forgive and welcome you with
open arms His way.
One choice began a long descent to
darkness that will blind;
One choice can again light the way for
you the truth to find.
The devil's power is to deceive; that you
simply have no choice.
But God gives power to believe and gives
you back your voice.
Your Father true will value you when earthly parents cause a rift.
Your Father true will welcome you when once you return to Him.
All that's required is to believe that you can return to Him.
Then all that you're created for can quickly be reborn.
Your broken heart will surely mend, no longer lost, forlorn.
You'll find new life with peace and joy beyond all you've ever known.
While angels in heaven now rejoice, the devil's glee has flown.
Who are you?
You can tell.
Child of heaven,
Or slave of hell.
By His Spirit; not at all what I used to be.

MARRIAGE

One woman, one man
Was always His plan.
Full intimacy could set each one free,
Yet pride had its way, for each wanted his say,
Not to fully accept. First, the woman had wept.
Then, the man went away. Now, neither could stay.
They were not made the same; let the difference remain.
Let full marriage be one when each learns to have fun,
Seeing each other's ways yet learning to praise,
Not counting their faults, nor hiding in vaults.
Your "you" is so great that my "me" cannot wait
For new discovery of what you are to me.
Not wanting lots more, just accepting, before
Forgetting your own, then love blossoms full-blown.
I know you, you know me, God gives discovery.
Man intended to learn what he never could earn,
For grace was the key; "I'm so glad you're not me."
If it's coffee for you, it's tea for me.
Yet when each has his way, a shared vision has sway.
You have learned; you've not earned
A copy of you that would never do.
How better could God give humans His nod,
Each forgetting himself to inherit God's wealth.
Yet when two become one, they've begun to have fun.
Sad is better than mad; laughter seldom is bad.

We can laugh at others yet forget all are brothers.
All are sisters, too, sensitive to prove
We can laugh at what's true, both for me and for you.
Our God laughs; so can we.
Maybe after, we see.

ONE FAMILY

By many hands, the board was spread; the feast was simple fare.
And many paused to share a smile,
and many paused for prayer.
As gleeful antics of the young received a strong reproof,
Light laughter sheltered elder sins in
gentler love of truth.
Communal was the mood that hour, and
God was surely there.
All years gone by were blended in,
all pain with joy to spare.
The mantle cloth was not brocade,
and spills were not unknown,
But napkins offered all around absorbed
both spills and frowns.
The tales that bloomed were friendly guests,
bouquet of fragrant creed.
No hostile seed, brewed hemlock strong,
reproached a generous deed.
The slightest scent will satisfy when
faded blooms bloom still.
The rarest spice can't rectify what bitter thoughts distill.
The generations gather in, content in peace to dine,
A balancing of yours and mine,
unbound by blood, but kin.
Where are such families to be found,
by will of fate still stable?
Wherever welcome still abounds for
strangers at the table.

TRUE MARRIAGE

Why forego sex now?
For the sake of your vow!
If you first learn how to wait,
You won't be quick to deviate.
Once you've chosen marriage trust,
You won't go quickly into lust.
Your mate will sooner trust your pledge
If you're not one to jump the hedge.
There are many reasons more,
For you not to simply score.
Having many partners makes your risk great,
Disease spreads among those who don't hesitate.
AIDS became a most deadly kiss.
Homosexual dates risked all for bliss.
When the idea of marriage was then borrowed,
Still, previous patterns promoted sorrow.
Even biblical marriage is subject to heal.
DNA tests now reveal the real.
When a parent was not the original source,
The child will wonder who, of course.
Adoptions are never quite the same
Since a lust to know the truth remains.
Children are gifts from the Father on high,
Bringing richness to marriage none can deny.

WHAT IS LOVE

In love, no matter how far you roam, you still have the choice to go
back home.
The truest love between man and wife is total commitment
throughout their life.
Men and women were made for each other.
Without birth, no man would have a brother.
Love tells of amazing grace
That teaches forgiveness to our race.
When God Himself took the form of a man, He came to earth as
His divine plan.
Forecast by prophets where and when in fullness of time to
Bethlehem.
Many turned from sin to belief that the God of love can bring
relief.
From the lures of the devil who is real, but who exists, proving love
can reveal
A way out of pain from our wrong choice,
For true freedom means we've been given a voice.
It's the truth that sets you free; the devil hates all liberty.
True love provides the way back home, no matter how far we
choose to roam.
When has it been that the blind can see?
When Jesus comes to set them free.
When has it been that the deaf can hear?
Love makes clear and banishes fear.
Self-sacrifice is not easy for men,
But has the most power in the end.

God was at one time crucified,
But His Word has never died.
His spirit is here when men choose love.
He lives within and takes us above
All the chains that enslave
And saves us from the grave.
Love endures forevermore:
Eternity is at the door.
Many we have lost in death
Can be found again.
For those who embrace true love,
Death is not the end.

A SOLDIER'S LAMENT

✍

I was a private
Who knew what it meant
To serve under men who knew they were sent.
George Washington prayed for our safety and zeal,
Well-knowing that our God
Could protect and was real.
How glorious now,
For a general denial,
Of God's primary place when faith is on trial!
How sad is the fate
Of men under his rule,
For men without God,
Face an enemy cruel,
Who divides both men's souls
And a country once whole.
Repent being the tool
Of the media's self-imposed rule.
When such leaders repent,
As their soldiers lament,
Faith can be restored;
God no longer ignored.

DECLARATION OF DEPENDENCE ON GOD

We do not give away our health
For the seeking of Big Pharma's wealth.
Forcing our military to take the shot
Is a right you certainly have not.
We have seen how far you'll go
To risk potential side effects
For those sworn to defeat foes!
What if the foe is now within?
That simply means the reach of sin
Has gone far too far to endure
For those whose patriotism is pure
The military sworn to defend us
Has now got to defend public trust
Government power has now turned sour
No more dishonorable discharge
For those whose president takes charge
He has proven we would not choose
a leader who wrongly thinks
it's our own soldiers we should lose
Let's recheck election results
To save ourselves from more insults
Our military needs to be fit for war
Not recovering from shots many abhor.
When shots are fired from within
We have a country to defend.
In God we trust; If die we must.
Heaven is nearby: Let the eagle fly.

DID YOU KNOW?

∽

"Militaryatheist.org" is an actual website,
Which reports chaplains who spread the light.
Soldiers are dedicated, but to what?
To leftist slogans that try to shut
Off the best our faith can offer?
Instead of prayer, they want more coffers:
A death that seems the end of life,
When Christians know that life is strife.
For the sake of better beliefs
That can bring to death relief:
Not worldly woes but God-sent bliss
That atheists will surely miss.
Do not let their threats prevail.
Christians have always chosen jail
Over agreement with deadly lies
That say God's Word should be despised.
Obama as our commander-in-chief
Sent the following directive about belief:
"Religious proselytization is not
Permitted in the Department of Defense."
Look at our history to see if that makes sense!
George Washington directed those in charge:
Appoint chaplains to encourage prayers at large.
We needed God to overcome oppression
And so fought for a country without repression
Of the beliefs that gave us liberty.
For God's Word is the key to set men free,
Free from life as personal gain,

Free from dictates that seem insane,
To those who know where true peace is found
After all the fighting on the ground.
Our soldiers must be free to pray
For God's strength is ours
When we follow His way.
Down with directives limiting faith indeed,
Victory comes: let truth sustain our creed.
God says to share the truth far and wide.
We obey God, not man when he decides.

MARINE SING-A-LONG

A tribute to Marine Stuart Scheller,
Imprisoned voice for those who died,
Whose leaders' silence falsified.
All control from the top!
What a colossal flop!
We do not intend to lose
The freedom for each one to choose
Nor freedom for valid votes to count,
Not allowing mail-in fraud to mount.
All creators should be free:
One good idea brings victory.
But let's be sure the truth prevails
And double-check results that fail.
Those bent on securing their own places
Won't serve the best for any races.
Those who choose to serve others instead
Will honor the heritage won by the dead,
Who risked their lives for freedom's sake,
Who suffered for the right to take
Charge of their own children's lives—
Not subjecting them to a godless state
That cares not for the unborn's fate.

MEMORIAL DAY, MEMORIAL DAY

∽

I knew him as the Daddy
Who had to stay away.
But when I grew, it was then I knew
That absent fathers still are true,
That absent fathers have a calling
To keep their country safe from falling,
That absent fathers far away
Have duties, so they cannot stay.
But there is hope of a returning,
For which the smallest child is yearning.
Daddy far will still come home
To treasure times they do not roam,
To treasure wives who day to day
Pray for their safety while away,
To treasure children who are glad
When they finally greet their "missing" Dad,
To treasure all that they preserve
When traveling far with manly nerve,
To keep the safety zone drawn tight
Against the dangers they must fight.
Memorial Day, Memorial Day,
The soldiers leave that we may stay.
Yes, soldiers leave that we may stay
To celebrate Memorial Day.

THE MEN IN BLUE

We are the faithful. We are the true.
We serve in peace. We serve in war.
We plunge into fires. We leave fear behind.
We save the victims of sky-born design.
We run in by our calling when others run far.
When towers are falling, we are the prey.
We keep our calm in the midst of the fray.
We are New York PD. We serve night and day.
We know public service. We come as one.
My brothers and sisters have all joined the force;
A family tradition of service in course.
We keep the peace. We do not flee war.
In times of disaster, we come to the fore.
We are the servants to others in need.
We are the saviors when Christ needs our seed.
We're not cops and robbers, as shown on TV.
Our service speaks during difficulty.
We know Whom we serve, and God gives us our nerve.
The towers will fall, but our jobs are our call.
Skins of black, brown, and white are one in the fight.
When others run away, we stay.
A tribute.

GARGLE AND GO ON

I'm not one to give advice,
But I know some things that will suffice:
A hug a day is better than no hug at all,
Fear is of the enemy and leads to your fall,
Bad emotions are born from bad thoughts,
A lot of bad thinking comes from bad oughts.
We ought to stay at home and be hermits
Rather than daring to be bold like Kermit.
Even a fake frog on a TV show
Can show us a better way to go.
Live life with love as the perfect way,
But love merely romantic won't save the day.
Love that leads you to give a helping hand
Means you have to be open to walking the land.
You have to be open to meeting your neighbor.
You have to be open to trusting your Savior.
He is the greatest Healer of all,
Far better than hearing some demon's call.
Hide and be hidden—lose half of life.
For when you're not sleeping, you should face the strife
Of simply living a full life day by day,
Not retiring to shadows that won't light your way.
Gargle and then go on.
Get rid of your germs before they are born.

HUMAN TRAFFICKING

Do you not see the plea lost in my eye when you close your own
and allow no reply?
You care not to learn of my gifts and dreams; I am but the pawn of
your cruel schemes.
You think I belong to none but you, for slavery of children is easy
to do. We are the weak who are bound by your will, for no food is
given until— until.
I am but a boy who should grow to a man, yet I'm bound by fear to
obey your command.
All of my sisters are slaves just like me, with no smiles in their eyes
for the nightmare to be.
I dream of no mother, for I know not her care;
I dream of no father, for he is not there.
How should I care, who have been robbed of care?
How should I share, who am naked and bare?
How should I know love when it's only abuse?
How should I know faith when I'm human refuse?
How to look to the future when it's more of the same?
How do I protest if I'm given the blame?
All that's wrong is my fault, and the "love" will not halt.
I but sit here and stare and hear only "beware!"
I have no tears left, for there's no more to lose.
My childhood is gone, for I never could choose.
If your God has mercy, where is mercy for me?

LAMENT FOR AFGHANISTAN

Truly Afghanistan needs a helping hand.
The USA built upon freedom's base,
But then refused to take a stand,
Now all the progress goes to waste.

We surrendered arms to the Taliban
Rather than saving the U.S. brand.
We surrendered airfields and planes as well
So that native fighters faced new hell.
Brought by a foe that closed most schools,
Claiming female teachers could not rule.
What a disgrace for a country that leads
To leave their friends to a force that bleeds
And sacrifices Christians to a ban
By Sharia's law that claims Moslems can
Murder those who leave the Moslem fold,
Though murder is forbidden by our God of old.
The Bible stands as God's Word in the Quran,
Muhammad's Jewish wife led him to understand.
Twenty-five years of life with one Jewish wife
Had led him to believe the Jewish Word.
Though he did not read well, he gladly heard
That his Creator guides all those who fast and pray.
So, Mohammed sought the truth by night and day
Yet the truth of God changes not through the years.
The early Quran says no forcing of belief,
But militant Moslems try to rule by fear.

Clearly change came about with no relief,
Though the truth of God changes not year by year.
What changes is the mind of man,
And those who follow not God's plan.
The devil easily claims all space
When the Word of God can be erased.
Truly Afghanistan needs a helping hand.
The USA built upon freedom's base,
But then refused to take a stand,
Now all the progress goes to waste.

OBJECTION TO REJECTION

Insurance adjusters are given rules, but we can object or look like fools.
The time for petitions we can no longer defer; to show agreement
for justice, we would prefer
Since no exceptions can now be made
To government rules that seem bought and paid.
It's time for a more democratic view
For the sake of owners who should have rights, too.
We've paid car insurance for years on end,
But now find a limit to what they will spend.
If your injured car's deemed over-age,
Its value is decreased by blue book page.
It does not matter the record of care,
Nor how long-cherished, as mileage would share
The car can be totaled with no appeal.
This is truly injustice that seems like a steal.
Regulations for insurance say it is trash,
And the only help is minimal cash
That will not buy a car as good
As the one they could repair if they would.
A few extra thousand could preserve a great car
Versus not enough refund to buy one on par.
It is time for allowance of exceptions to rules.
Otherwise, rules give no allowance for tools
That are perfectly able to return cars to jewels.
If inside structures must be welded,
That is part of repair that should not be gelded

By the unfair limit of one "sacred" blue book that doesn't allow
justice a second look.
If a car still runs well, it should not be sent to auto hell!

THE WORLD IS WATCHING

As the bombings continue
The world reacts anew.
Russia is writing death.
Their children now bereft
Of pride by power misused.
The news may be confused,
Yet children will remember
One man led them to surrender
All pride through Russian genocide.
Now freedoms cause can't be denied.
True power belongs to those who know
Propaganda never will truth bestow.
God's truth writes men's minds as one.
True unity has now begun.
Mere control from the top
Proves a colossal flop.

TO FLORIDA POWER AND LIGHT

On the occasion of replacing human representatives:
Thank you, FPL, for joining the trend.
Machines over people will then be your end.
Why promote human contact
When machines are the best,
When you prefer machinery to humans,
You have failed the test.
Machines never break down,
But is this the case?
Machines never miss work,
But all thought is erased.
Machines never smile, so they seem so secure.
They will never make friends, so you can endure.
You eliminate all traces of trying to be kind.
Your windows now empty will no appeal find.
Your machines will not fix all your problems by far.
Machines only show how money managed you are.
To be illustrated in the following way:
Someone at the window acting like a robot says,
"But don't you understand?"
When the person protests and
Wants to see the manager,
Another robot shows up.

ENGLISH IS FOR THE BRAVE

Don't worry. Trump donors can stand for some shame,
Since others detest them when they're not to blame.
What's right has been turned so far upside down
By those who kill babies with never a frown.
What's wrong is that truth has been blasted by lies,
And too many believe what the media spies.

English is truly for the brave.
We'll believe it's possible to be saved.
If we refuse to be bound like a slave,
Especially by our government,
It's socialism we resent.
"Those are laws
Just because"
Doesn't sit well with us
Since the US won't sit
In the back of the bus.
Democrats ruled the South
When that rule was made.
(But they like to accuse others
of the stuff they portrayed.)
Republicans aren't innocent, either,
But this poem is done;
So, let's take a breather.

GRAPES OF WRATH

Filipinos first started the strike
Against grape growers who would not hike
Wages for pickers in their fields
Since better conditions might curb their yields.
No health or injury benefits came,
Even for men working years for the same
Long, tiring hours with skillful hands,
Who lived without wives or retirement plans.
Men could emigrate but not their counterparts,
Nor could they marry white wives with good hearts.
At last, Mexicans began to arrive.
Both sexes were allowed to cross borders to thrive
Yet a problem soon became severe.
Couples formed, but the strike could disappear.
Mexicans were hired to replace others who quit,
But Filipinos saw brothers who were fit
To join in their strike for better wages.
So joint rewards could come in stages,
Closer to the American way of life
Since they had worked long with no strife,
Even lacking hope of family or wife.
Brotherhood ties had become so strong
That Mexicans could also feel their wrong.
Together they chose not to continue
Working just for owners' revenue,
Sharing the wealth was clearly right.

Grapes unpicked were a pitiful sight
Yet far more pitiful in the eyes of many
Were laborers whose blood and sweat made pennies.
Concerned citizens saw a better way
To let the people have their say:
A strike against buying grapes won out,
For the rights of many have more clout
Than gains of growers who planted once,
And then treated a worker as a dunce
To sacrifice so many long hours,
Just to enrich land owners' bowers.
Both strikes led to fairness and success
Against grape buying, as well as worker stress.
United with citizens who saw their plight,
Farm workers won better wages as a right.

THE SEAL OF THE SPIRIT

We have but one God, Creator of all earth.
The same Jesus came through one human birth.
We become one with the seal of the Spirit:
God returns to His children, gives us His merit.
God with us and in us, a transforming joy,
His Holy Spirit, our best thoughts employ.
Oh Lord God, you've given us all your best,
The seal of Your Spirit has given us rest.
We strive no longer but live in Your will,
For good comes from sorrow, from trials for sure.
In giving to others, we serve You each day,
For Your strength becomes ours when we follow Your way.
You've shown us the way to endure all our fate.
In forgiving all wrongs, we are freed from their weight.
Death is but the door; Your full glory awaits.
The seal of His Spirit is God living within;
We are His in our living, we are His at our end.

HR1, AND THOSE LIKE IT, SHOULD NOT BE LAW

༄

As the wave of e-mails continued to mount,
Why should locals protest that dead voters don't count?
As the wave of ballots by truckloads arrived,
The deadline was extended so late voters could thrive.
Since COVID-19 restrictions hampered fair votes as before,
Those late ballots were perfect weapons of war.
Now Congress reveals proof in HR1
That the battle had only just begun.
Congress is proposing federal control,
So illegal votes can be legally whole.
What about states' rights for local oversight?
What about the electoral college to preserve local rights?
Without the college, only states with high populations
Would totally take over rule of this nation.
Our founders had wisdom to preserve minority rights,
But without the college, we'd be in a plight:
California, Texas, New York, and Florida, too,
Could swamp smaller states in a tidal wave of blue.
But Florida stands out with better control,
Able to monitor all unjust polls.
Thanks to Governor Ron DeSantis' wisdom
We have Florida freedom: check out all who come,
Wishing to vote with IDs in hands;
So, we hamper illegal votes by brigands.
Thank goodness for the power of state control,
Now others are moving here to remain whole.

Thank goodness for a veteran at the helm of our ship;
So, all other vets know their freedom won't slip
Into the hands of the few that would take
Away all the power that belongs to each state.
When patriots vote down HR1,
The defeat of the unjust has finally begun.
Florida knows that Trump won the election there
By 371,686 votes, since the election was fair.
HR1 wants to ruin local control
By having the feds run all of our polls.
It also aspires to steal taxpayer funds
To finance incumbent campaigns, leaving others undone.
What a way to ruin fair elections forever
By giving feds unjust power to be clever,
By making legal through HR1,
All the deceptions that had just begun.
Democracy means the people are free
From socialist control over liberty.

ILLEGAL LAWS

It's your business—It's your town; why risk God's divine frown?
The Bible clearly says usury's a crime: limit interest to 10 percent a dollar or only a dime.
Those who blatantly charge 15 percent will wonder where their blessings went.
God has guidelines for the right, but there were lobbyists in the night.
During Sunday school-teaching Carter's reign, our protective law disappeared for gain.
Our 10 percent limit on interest had divine cover, but illegal laws now more profit recover.
Usury meant a limit of 10 percent; now, 25 percent is the common bent.
How did we vote in legal theft?
Man's greed decreed we were bereft of laws God gave to protect His people When men blatantly disgrace their steeple.
Have they even read the Bible at all?
Know that divine law prevents your fall,
But men blatantly seek the fall of all.
Charging interest gives debtors no thrill,
For debt quadruples in monthly bills.
Every dollar borrowed "earns" a quarter,
Not the dime limit God decrees for barter.
People wonder where their money went.
If you charge one dollar, you pay 25 percent.

God clearly calls it illegal theft.
But by man's law, you are bereft.
The Bible clearly limits interest for a loan,
Only 10 percent per payment to atone;
Any more is an illegal law,
Promoted by thieves you never saw.

SOCIAL DIVISION WITH PRECISION

We have an enemy here on earth,
Who claims brotherhood is determined by birth.
Those who consider skin color their clue
To decide the basis for friendship's glue
Have never learned all men are brothers.
Belief in God's brotherhood recovers
All from the lies of separation,
Purged at the founding of our nation.
Slaves had existed long before Christ came.
The chosen Jews had centuries of the same
Yet once God came down in self-sacrifice,
Many understood that slaves won't suffice.
To bear the burden of toil, all should share
Yet beliefs were divided; some didn't care.
Our nation was founded with new beliefs
That God made all equal; slavery like a thief.
Yet, it took a time of civil war
To end a practice that existed before:
Still, belief in slavery did not yet end;
Instead, men invented the socialist trend.
Based on men like Marx and Mao
Who believed private property should go,
Slavery then, in disguise, reappeared.
For when individuals do not earn their goods,
And all is distributed "to all" by hoods,
There are no believers in truth to lead.

Leaders who distribute will rule all creeds.
Leaders can lie, steal, kill and destroy,
Just as the devil leads his toys.
Everyone in the masses must not complain,
Or punishment comes with death and pain.
Slavery, of all, is the socialist call.
How can rulers be pure, controlling all public booths?
Dishonest voting destroys all truths.
How can rulers distribute who want to own all,
And have a nation of slaves at their beck and call?
If you no longer believe in the morals of God,
You confiscate all shoes others had shod,
You nationalize business since you rule all the rods,
And votes do not matter because they do the count.
And they make the media results that mount,
A false belief in all results
That maintains their newfound cults.
Private property lets men own what worked they for—not the state,
But socialism lets rulers divide and decide all your fate.
Christians have morals to guide their choices,
But socialists lie, bribe and control all voices.
Who owns the media?
Just check and see.
It's all propaganda, so you won't be free.
Would you trust leaders who lie and steal?
Then, realize the slavery you'll get is real.
Isn't it great that all would be equal slaves?
But the few at the top escape all that depraves.

TERM LIMITS NOW

Time for an American powwow.
We are on the warpath now.
Term limits for Congress are our vow.
Enough of salaries near 200 grand!
No more retirement to beat the band!
The COVID-19 bills even gave them a raise.
How many think such greed should be praised?
Limit senators to two terms fast
Before we forget justice in our past.
Limit reps to four terms with no bail,
With no more perks to tip the scale.
Let's nix tax dollars to pay off their campaigns.
They really do think that money rains.
Other campaigners would be on their own,
With far less chance to claim their throne.
Democracy demands we vote many out,
So new tribes have their own say with a shout.
Let new tribes come forth who won't take bribes.
That's biblical truth that God describes.
No wonder prayers were banned in schools.
Some promote a different set of rules.
Let's return to service for our land.
So our American dream still stands.

WHY YOU SHOULD RUN FOR CONGRESS

⁂

Would you like full pay for part-time work?
Then look at Congress as a perk.
Americans carry a full-time load,
Two hundred and forty days clocking in from the road.
But Congress schedules 124 days a year,
Then it's safe to disappear.
From 1785 to 1815, the pay was $6 per day,
Then it was raised by $8 for part-time pay.
That lasted till 1855—just think
What they needed to survive.
Then your grandparents were still alive.
Now Congressional pay has gone fast track,
And it doesn't seem there's looking back.
And this was for only a few months a year,
What "minimal wage" should call forth a tear.
Because really, they only deserve just one
Since the wage hike has begun.
Now they average $174,000 per year,
But remember, for half the year, they disappear.
They can earn extra money the rest of the time,
Up to another 15 percent and health care prime.
Total package is $200,000 per year;
So, they are the rich they pretend to fear.
(Every member of Congress earns more than 97 percent of Americans.)
They are in the top 3 percent.
Now, do you see why you should repent?

Why haven't you run for office yet?
You could do better than most. It's a bet.
The Corona Relief Bill
Contained a congressional raise.
How many think such greed should be praised?
We can throw most of the incumbents out.
For fiscal conservatives, we'll give a shout
Let's go back to a budget that's balanced
Since spending is the congressional talent!
Since their gift is to overspend,
They devalue our dollar in the end.
Vote for those who'll limit congressional terms.
We should share the wealth, not hoard our germs.

DEATH INCORPORATED

Planned Parenthood is running scared:
their budgets have been sadly pared.
They now send letters of appeal
because their true concern is real.
Loss of life has been their business,
as the sale of body parts will witness.
How much they depend on income stream!
Mothers must pay for each loss extreme.
Then having no reverence for the death of
those whose lungs never took a breath,
Managers seek a full-term abortion,
increasing profit to higher proportions.
Calculate prices for livers and hearts:
demand is rising for baby parts,
But just remember the public good:
population control for the neighborhood.
Especially neighborhoods chosen with care:
who would want more babies there?
Do you ever wonder how much care they take?
Do they offer to pay for any mistake?
Do they offer support for mothers who wonder whether their
babies have become plunder?
Do they give counsel to those left behind who finally regret having
been blind?

Do they help to heal the hearts of the mothers, who cannot forget
the thought of the other? Mothers may meet their babies in heaven,
but many live with regrets seven times seven.
All of this suffering comes with a price:
You are paying for human sacrifice.

www.ingramcontent.com/pod-product-compliance
Lightning Source LLC
Chambersburg PA
CBHW051226120626
46547CB00013B/1525